KU-719-730

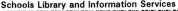

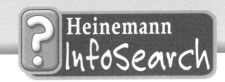

WHY SHOULD I WASH?

✦ and other questions about keeping clean

and healthy ✦

Louise Spilsbury

www.heinemann.co.uk/library
Visit our website to find out more information about **Heinemann Library** books.

To order:
 Phone 44 (0) 1865 888066
 Send a fax to 44 (0) 1865 314091
 Visit the Heinemann Bookshop at www.heinemann.co.uk/library to browse our catalogue and order online.

First published in Great Britain by Heinemann Library, Halley Court, Jordan Hill, Oxford OX2 8EJ, part of Harcourt Education. Heinemann is a registered trademark of Harcourt Education Ltd.

Editorial: Nancy Dickmann, Jennifer Tubbs and Louise Galpine
Design: David Poole and Tokay Interactive Ltd (www.tokay.co.uk)
Illustrations: Kamae Design Ltd
Picture Research: Rebecca Sodergren and Liz Eddison
Production: Séverine Ribierre and Jonathan Smith

Originated by Ambassador Litho Ltd
Printed in China by Wing King Tong

ISBN 0 431 11092 1
07 06 05 04 03
10 9 8 7 6 5 4 3 2 1

British Library Cataloguing in Publication Data
Spilsbury, Louise
Why Should I Wash? and other questions about keeping clean and healthy
613.4
A full catalogue record for this book is available from the British Library.

Acknowledgements
Corbis pp. **6** (David Woods), **7** (Layne Kennedy), **11** (Ed Bock); Getty Images pp. **4** (Imagebank), **22**; Science Photo Library pp. **8**, **9**, **10**, **12**, **23**, **24**, **26**; Tudor Photography pp. **5**, **13**, **14**, **15**, **16**, **17**, **18**, **19**, **21**, **25**, **27**, **28**.

Cover photograph of child washing hands, reproduced with permission of Tudor Photography.

The publishers would like to thank Julie Johnson for her assistance in the preparation of this book.

Every effort has been made to contact copyright holders of any material reproduced in this book. Any omissions will be rectified in subsequent printings if notice is given to the publishers.

CONTENTS

Words appearing in the text in bold, **like this**, are explained in the Glossary.

WHY SHOULD I WASH?

Washing may seem like just another chore, but did you know that washing is the single most important thing you can do to prevent catching **infections**? Washing is the best way to stop **germs** from spreading, and some germs can make you ill.

Where do germs come from?

Germs are living things so tiny that you can only see them through a microscope. There are germs everywhere around us – in soil, in water, in the air, on our pets and in our food. Many germs are harmless or even useful, and we could not survive in a world without germs. Other germs cause infectious diseases, such as colds, flu and diarrhoea, if they get into your body.

There are germs in soil, and this is why gardeners usually wear gloves. If you touch your mouth with muddy fingers, you may pass germs into your body.

How do germs get inside me?

Your skin is like armour. It is made up of skin **cells** filled with a tough substance called **keratin**. This protective layer covers almost all of your whole body. Most germs cannot get through healthy skin – they can only infect you if they get in through an opening in your skin, such as your mouth or nose.

Imagine that a friend has a cold. They sneeze and do not cover their mouth. Germs fly on to the desk. When you touch the desk, some of the germs rub on to your fingers. At break time, you put your fingers into your mouth when you eat a snack. Some of the germs move from your fingers to the inside of your body. Now you risk catching the cold.

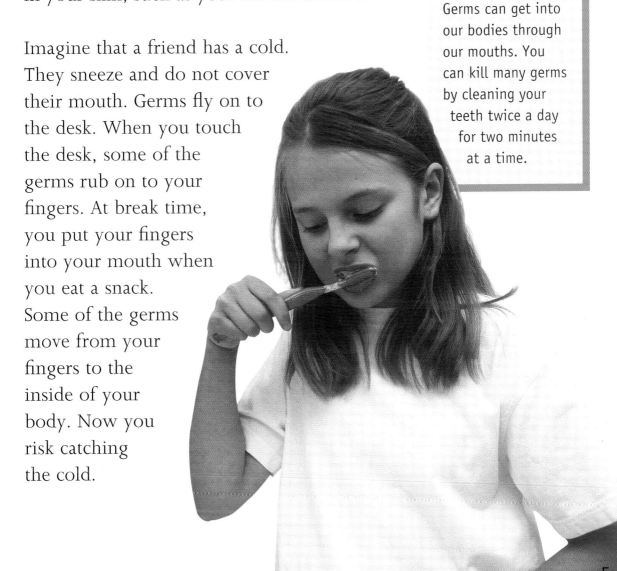

Germs can get into our bodies through our mouths. You can kill many germs by cleaning your teeth twice a day for two minutes at a time.

How does washing help?

Most **germs** spread through contact. They rub on to your fingers from doorknobs or food, or mix with sweat and dirt on your body. Washing with warm, soapy water gets rid of most germs. Bits of soap attach themselves to any particles of dust, dirt and germs so, when you rinse off the soap, these things get washed down the plughole, too.

Pets, such as cats, seem like clean animals because they are always washing themselves, but their saliva (spit) contains lots of germs. Always wash your hands after stroking animals.

WHEN SHOULD I WASH MY HANDS?

You should wash your hands:
- before eating or preparing food
- before you treat a cut or wound
- after using the bathroom
- after touching or playing with pets or other animals
- after playing outside or gardening
- after coughing, sneezing or blowing your nose
- after handling rubbish.

Cleaning wounds is important. Covering larger cuts keeps them clean.

What if I cut myself?

Germs can also get into your skin when there is a hole in your skin – such as a cut. Cuts bleed because there are blood vessels just below the surface of the skin. If germs get into cuts, they can travel around your body very quickly in your blood. If a cut bleeds, press a clean, soft cloth on it until the bleeding stops. Then wash the wound with clean, warm water. After drying the cut, you can rub antibacterial cream on it, which kills germs. Wash your hands first, and apply cream with a swab to keep the wound clean.

If a wound was caused by an animal's claws or teeth or by something especially dirty, ask a doctor to check it out, because **bacteria** from these things can cause serious **infections**.

HOW ARE GERMS BAD FOR ME?

All **germs** are tiny living things that take in food, give off waste, grow, reproduce (make more living things like themselves) and die. When some germs live inside people, they can make us ill. The four commonest types of germs are **bacteria**, **viruses**, **fungi** and **protozoa**.

What are bacteria like?

Different kinds of bacteria live in different ways. Most bacteria are harmless and some are useful, such as those that live in our **intestines** and help us to process our food. Yoghurt is

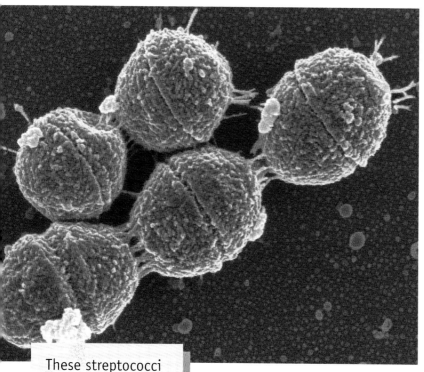

These streptococci bacteria cause sore throats. They have been magnified over 170,000 times their actual size.

healthy to eat because of the bacteria it contains. A small percentage of bacteria, however, can cause us problems, such as sore throats, tonsillitis, tooth decay, ear **infections**, pneumonia and tetanus.

Viruses

Viruses are even tinier than bacteria. Almost all viruses cause disease. They spread quickly through your body and make you sick. Diseases spread by viruses include chicken pox, flu, mumps and measles.

Fungi

Some fungi have many **cells**, and others are tiny and have just one cell. Like other germs, fungi live on other living things, particularly in damp, warm places. Only about half of all fungi types cause disease in humans, such as athlete's foot. Penicillin is a helpful fungus that is used as an **antibiotic** to destroy bacteria.

Protozoa

Protozoa are germs with one cell that usually live in water. Few kinds of protozoa cause disease in people, and they are usually passed on in dirty water. Some protozoa cause infections in the intestine, such as dysentery.

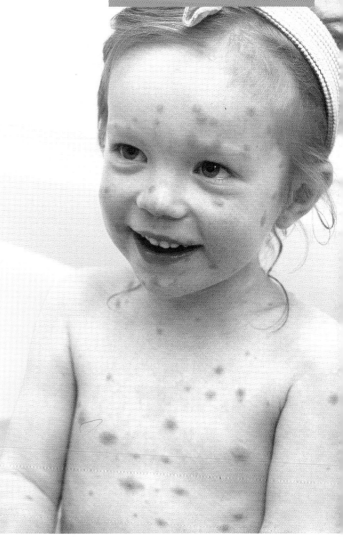

Chicken pox is an infectious disease that most people catch during childhood. It is caused by a virus.

How do germs hurt us?

Our bodies are made up of millions of tiny building blocks, called **cells**. When germs get into your cells, they live there. They take in **nutrients** and **energy** from your cells, leaving them weaker. The germs also produce waste, called toxins. These toxins are like poisons in your system and they make you ill.

This picture shows a white blood cell (coloured blue and purple) attacking **bacteria** (coloured yellow) inside a person's blood. The cells have been greatly magnified so we can see this happening.

Does my body attack germs?

Your body has its own defences against germs – your **immune system**. When germs invade your blood system, your blood quickly recognizes that chemicals on the germs, called antigens, are not part of your body. White blood cells in your blood make chemicals called **antibodies**, which attach themselves to the germs. This helps other white blood cells to seek out the invaders and to move in to destroy them.

How do medicines help?

If your body is unable to fight off the germs, you may need to see a doctor. Doctors can tell which germs have invaded your body by looking at the germs in samples of your blood. Then they match the medicine to the germ. Medicines are made up of chemicals that are safe for your body cells, but which attack a weakness in the germs inside your cells.

If you have to take medicine to cure an infection, make sure that you take exactly the amount prescribed by the doctor.

IN THE PAST

In the past, before people understood that germs could pass on diseases, many people died from **infectious** diseases, such as cholera and typhoid. In 19th-century England, a surgeon called Joseph Lister encouraged doctors to wash their hands regularly and to use clean equipment. Being clean reduced the number of infections being spread by germs a lot!

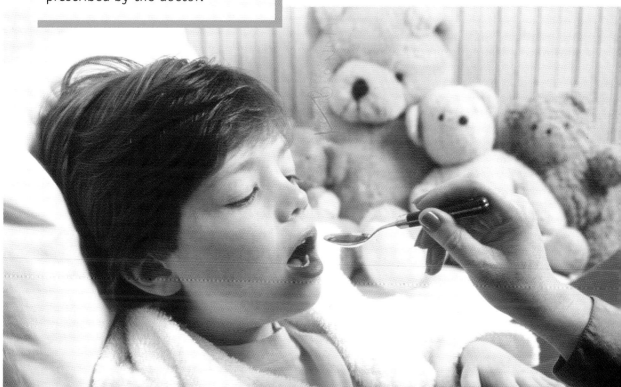

HOW OFTEN SHOULD I WASH?

There are no hard and fast rules about washing, because how often you wash depends, in part, on how dirty you get. However, even if you do not look dirty, you need to wash off sweat, dead flakes of skin and **germs** that you cannot see.

Shedding skin

Every day, you shed millions of dead skin **cells** from your skin. Skin cells move up from the bottom of the epidermis (top layer of your skin) to the top, collecting tough **keratin** as they go. When they reach the surface, they die – forming a protective outer layer – and new skin cells move up to replace them. When you rub your skin, some of the old dead skin cells fall off and become part of the dust that you see on furniture, or they rub off on to your clothes.

This picture shows greatly magnified skin cells. Taking a shower or bath every day washes away dead skin cells like these.

What is sweat?

When your body gets too hot, it sweats to cool itself down. You have sweat **glands** – body parts that make sweat – all over your body. They release sweat through the pores (tiny holes) in your skin. In the air, the sweat dries off your body, taking the warmth away and helping to cool you down.

Sweat is mostly made up of water, but it also contains chemicals such as ammonia, salts, sugar and urea (a form of waste left over when your body digests certain foods). Sweat does not smell. However, **bacteria** like to grow in warm, moist places, such as sweaty skin, and when they grow on sweat, unpleasant-smelling chemicals are released.

Sweat glands are more common in some parts of the body, such as your armpits, and that is why these parts get sweatier than others, and also why you need to wash them more often.

Why is my sweat starting to smell?

As you get older, you will notice that your sweat begins to smell more. This is because you are reaching puberty, the time of life when your body changes so that you can become an adult. Girls start puberty at any time between eight and fourteen years old, and boys between ten and seventeen years old. During puberty, your body starts to release a new substance from special sweat glands, called apocrine glands, found mainly under your armpits. Although this substance does not smell, it mixes with **bacteria** on your skin and causes an odour.

Some people use deodorant on their armpits after washing, to mask the smell of sweat.

WHAT IS BODY ODOUR?

Body odour is a mixture of smells, including:
- old sweat that bacteria feed on and then rot
- oils produced by your skin that collect and go stale
- dirt that gathers on your skin.

A daily routine

Although there are no rules about washing, it is best to get into good habits. Bacteria can quickly build up on parts of the body with many sweat glands, or where there are folds of skin, such as under the arms, where dirt is easily trapped but hard to see. Having a warm bath or shower each day or every other day is the easiest way to get rid of any bacteria. Using a clean soapy flannel or loofah helps to rub dirt off.

You can rub off healthy skin oils if you wash your face too much. Just wash it with soap or cleanser at night, and rinse it with warm water in the morning.

Drying yourself is an important part of washing! Use a clean towel and make sure that you are dry all over, especially in folds of skin and between your toes.

WHY SHOULD I WEAR CLEAN CLOTHES?

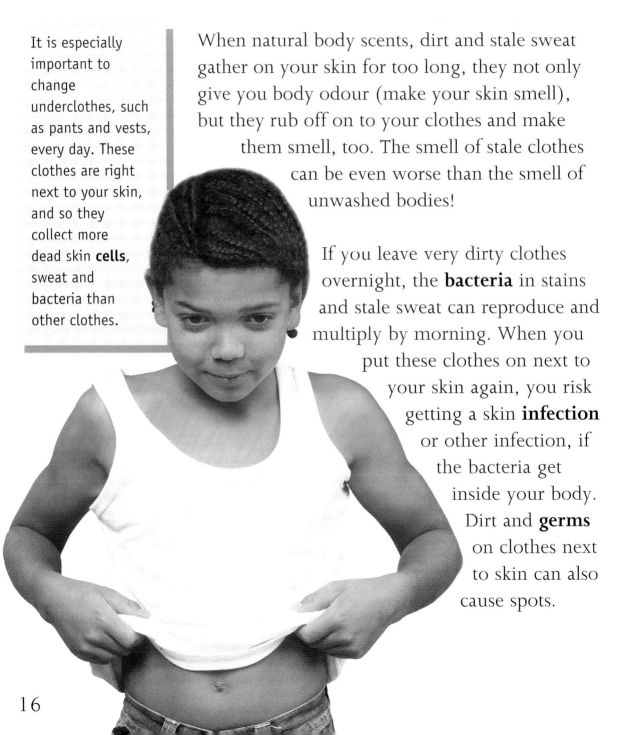

It is especially important to change underclothes, such as pants and vests, every day. These clothes are right next to your skin, and so they collect more dead skin **cells**, sweat and bacteria than other clothes.

When natural body scents, dirt and stale sweat gather on your skin for too long, they not only give you body odour (make your skin smell), but they rub off on to your clothes and make them smell, too. The smell of stale clothes can be even worse than the smell of unwashed bodies!

If you leave very dirty clothes overnight, the **bacteria** in stains and stale sweat can reproduce and multiply by morning. When you put these clothes on next to your skin again, you risk getting a skin **infection** or other infection, if the bacteria get inside your body. Dirt and **germs** on clothes next to skin can also cause spots.

Healthy clothes

Some kinds of fabrics or styles of clothing are healthier than others. Nylon and some other human-made fabrics tend to make you sweat more. Cotton fabric allows air through and helps to keep you fresher. On hot days, it is better to wear loose clothes, such as baggy T-shirts, which protect your skin from the sun, but allow air to get to your skin to keep you cool. Tight clothes are also more likely to collect sweat and become smelly more quickly.

Changing clothes for sport helps to keep you clean and healthy.

People change into special exercise clothes when they do sport, partly to be comfortable – T-shirts and leotards are made of stretchy fabric that is easy to move in, and shorts allow legs to move freely. They also change into sports kit so that they do not make their ordinary clothes dirty and sweaty.

WHY SHOULD I CHANGE MY SOCKS?

You have more sweat **glands** in your feet than anywhere else, and you spend a lot of time on your feet. When sweat soaks into your socks, **bacteria** soon multiply, because they thrive in the warm, damp darkness inside your shoes. That is why it is important to put fresh, clean socks on every day, and preferably after doing sports or exercise.

How else can I help my feet?

Keep your feet as clean and dry as possible. Wear cotton socks, and wear different shoes every other day if you can. Keep your shoes clean, too, by wiping off mud and dirt, to stop these things getting on to your feet. If trainers get stale and sweaty, they can be washed in the washing machine.

Changing shoes after school allows your school shoes to dry out in the air, reducing the amount of bacteria in them.

What is athlete's foot?

If you do not change your socks and keep your feet clean and dry, you can catch foot **infections**. Athlete's foot is a skin infection caused by a mould-like **fungus** that lives on the dead skin **cells** on your feet. It makes you itchy, red and sore between the toes, and gives you flaky skin. It is not only athletes who can get athlete's foot – it is usually passed on to other people in swimming pool changing rooms, where the fungus thrives on warm, damp floors.

You can treat athlete's foot with a fungus-destroying (fungicidal) powder. To avoid catching athlete's foot in the first place, wash your feet well and dry them carefully. Also, avoid sharing towels with other people, because the infection can spread this way, too.

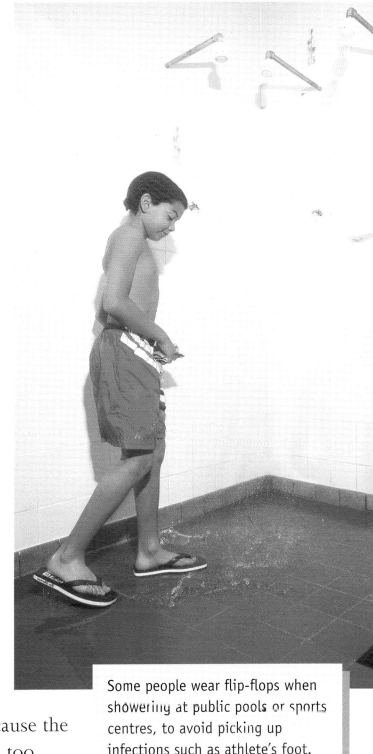

Some people wear flip-flops when showering at public pools or sports centres, to avoid picking up infections such as athlete's foot.

WHY SHOULDN'T I BITE MY NAILS?

Your fingernails have a vital job to do. They protect your fingertips, help you pick things up or to do things such as peel a grape. If you damage your nails, you damage your fingers' protection and leave them open to **infection**. This is especially so for those people who bite their nails to the quick and even make their fingers bleed.

Dirt and **germs** collect under your fingernails. When you bite your fingernails, you put your fingers in your mouth and let these germs into your body. Also, biting your nails makes them more likely to break and become infected – and it looks unpleasant.

Trim your nails using curved nail scissors or nail-cutters. When you cut, follow the curve of the nail, but do not cut nails too short.

How can I stop biting my nails?

The only real way to stop biting your nails is to be very determined. To help, you can buy a special clear nail polish, which tastes horrid. Some people give themselves a reward, such as a little present, for each week they manage to stop.

Looking after nails

Finger and toe nails need regular cleaning and trimming. Wash out dirt that collects under your nails when you wash your hands. Trim nails when they get too long, otherwise they crack and break, and this can make them feel sore. Also, your feet are growing all the time. If you do not cut your toe nails, your shoes will feel tight – and this is bad for growing feet.

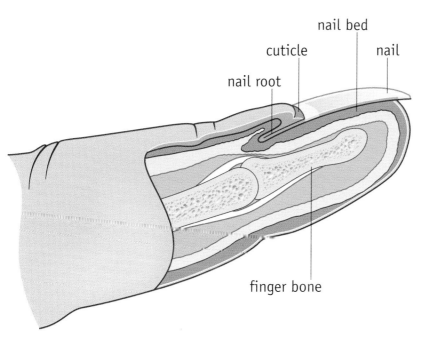

nail bed

cuticle   nail

nail root

finger bone

Cutting nails does not hurt, because nails do not contain any nerves – just dead **cells** filled with a tough substance called **keratin**. The only part that is alive and growing is the root, just under the surface.

21

WHY SHOULD I BLOW MY NOSE?

Because nose mucus contains germs and dirt or dust, you should blow it into a tissue to get rid of it.

Your nose is not just for smelling. It also contains hairs and a sticky liquid called mucus (snot), which catch little pieces of dust and dirt that you breathe in, to stop them getting inside your body. Blowing your nose helps to get rid of these **germs**.

Why does my nose run?

You always have a small amount of nose mucus. When you have a cold, you make extra mucus. It soaks up the germs and contains an **antiseptic** that helps to kill them. Mucus is usually clear but, when you have a cold, it often becomes green or thick and yellow because of the **bacteria**, dirt and dust in it. Your nose runs to get rid of this extra mucus.

Your nose is the first line of defence for your lungs, the vital body parts that control your breathing. The mucus and hair in your nose catch dust, dirt and bacteria particles to stop them travelling into your lungs, although bronchi (air tubes) in the lungs also contain some mucus to catch particles, too. If lungs become clogged with dirt or smoke, they do not work so well, and this can cause a range of problems with breathing.

WHY DO I SNEEZE?

If particles of dirt, dust or bacteria irritate the lining in your nose, you sneeze to get rid of them. First, your brain makes you take an extra big breath (the 'ah' part of 'ah-tishoo'!). Then your chest muscles squeeze your lungs, and air rushes out of you at high speed.

If you do not catch a sneeze, preferably in a tissue, you will pass on germs in mucus that sprays out at high speed.

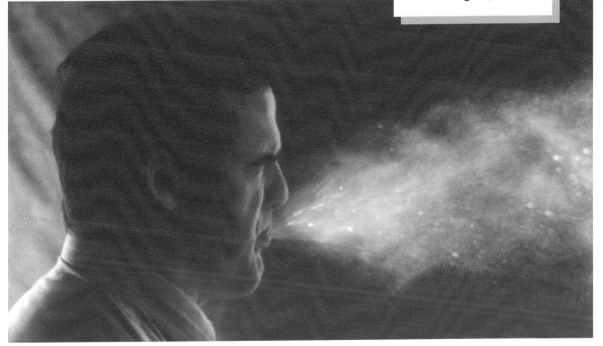

WHY SHOULD I WASH MY HANDS AFTER GOING TO THE BATHROOM?

It is especially important to wash your hands after going to the bathroom, because **germs** found in faeces (poo) can cause many illnesses. If you do not wash traces (tiny amounts) of faeces off your hands after you have wiped your bottom, they can be passed on – to other people and back to yourself.

Germs

Germs passed on through traces of faeces can cause diseases such as gastroenteritis, and can spread pinworms, which can live in human **intestines**. If traces of urine (wee) are not washed away, they can pass on **infections**. People who have mumps can pass on the infection through traces of their urine.

Tiny pinworm eggs can get into the body from traces of faeces. They hatch and live in the intestines. Your anus itches when the females lay eggs there. You can take medicine to get rid of them.

Bathroom hygiene

It is also important to wipe your bottom well after going to the bathroom. Girls should always wipe themselves from front to back. This stops **bacteria** from faeces around the **anus** being passed to the urethra (where urine comes out). It is also important to clean your bottom carefully every day when you bathe or shower. When washing, boys who have foreskin on their penis should gently draw that back and wash around the penis.

WASHING HANDS

It is important to wash your hands properly. You should:
- use soap and warm water running from the tap
- wash all parts of your hand thoroughly – including wrists, palms, the back of your hands, between your fingers and under your nails
- rub your hands together for at least 15 seconds
- dry carefully with a paper towel, hot air machine or clean towel.

Everyone should wash their hands after going to the bathroom. It takes less than a minute but it's very important.

25

WHY SHOULD I CLEAN MY ROOM?

Keeping yourself clean and healthy means keeping your surroundings clean and healthy, too. If your room gets dirty, **germs** will multiply and the number of tiny creatures that live amongst dust, such as dust mites, increases. It is normal and healthy to have some mites and bugs in your home, but you need to keep them under control by being clean.

This ferocious-looking dust mite is, in fact, only 0.3 mm long! You are only able to see it because it has been magnified (enlarged) many times.

What are dust mites?

Dust mites live in the dust that builds up in our homes – in bedding, soft toys and sofas. They are so small that we cannot see them without a microscope. They feed on tiny bits of skin that we shed every day, and that collect in dust on furniture and floors.

26

Keep dust mites down by dusting your room regularly with a damp cloth and hoovering often. Also, put clothes away. If you leave them lying around, they get dusty and dust mites live on them.

The dust mite's droppings are so light and tiny that they float in the air when you plump up a cushion or run across a carpet. When people with **asthma** or allergies breathe them in, they can cause unpleasant allergic reactions.

WHAT ARE ALLERGIES?

People have an allergy when their **immune system** reacts to something that is usually harmless to others. When the person comes into contact with an allergen (the thing they are allergic to), such as pet hair or dust, their immune system produces lots of **antibodies** to attack it. This releases chemicals called histamines, which make people feel unwell – giving them red, itchy eyes and sore skin, sneezing or even sickness and diarrhoea.

27

Can my pet come in my room?

Some people are allergic to pet hair. Even if you do not have allergies, it is important to clean up pet hair, because dead skin **cells** and saliva (spit) on it carry **germs**. You do not have to shut your pet out – just keep it clean and free from fleas, wash bedcovers that they lie on regularly and clean your room often.

What are bed bugs?

Have you ever heard the expression, 'Sleep tight, don't let the bed bugs bite'? Bed bugs are small insects that live in a mattress. They feed on tiny amounts of blood from people sleeping in the bed. Their bites itch and may cause an allergic reaction. Keeping your room and bed clean helps to keep out bugs and mites.

Keeping your room clean helps to keep you healthy and makes your room a pleasant place to be!

AMAZING FACTS

- You have about 7.5 million skin cells on every square centimetre of your body!

- Your skin is thickest on the palms and soles of your feet, and thinnest on your lips and around your eyes.

- One square centimetre of skin has about 100,000 **bacteria** on it. Many of these are harmless, and they take up space and food that would be filled by harmful bacteria if they were not there!

- Your saliva (spit) contains **antibodies** that destroy some of the **germs** that get into your mouth. We produce about a litre of saliva every day!

- Fingernails grow by about 1 millimetre a week.

- When you sneeze, air comes out of your nose at about 160 kilometres an hour – that is as fast as an express train!

- Eighty-five per cent of people who have **asthma** are allergic to dust mite droppings.

- An adult's feet can produce about an egg cup-full of sweat in a day.

GLOSSARY

antibodies   substances in the blood that protect the body by attacking germs

antiseptic   substance that destroys the germs that cause infection

anus   opening through which faeces leaves the body

asthma   when the lining of breathing tubes are easily irritated, so they become narrow and blocked with mucus, making it hard to breathe

bacteria   tiny living things found everywhere. Some bacteria can cause disease.

cell   smallest building block of living things

energy   energy allows living things to do everything they need to live and grow. Plants and animals make the energy they need from their food.

fungus   living thing that can be formed from a single cell or many cells. Some fungi cause disease. More than one fungus is called fungi.

germs   tiny living things that can cause disease

gland   part of the body that makes substances for use in the body or to be ejected from it

immune system   parts of the body that work together to defend it from disease

infection   kind of disease that can be caught by other people

intestines   hollow, coiled tubes near your stomach

keratin   kind of hard protein that forms hair and the outer layer of skin

nutrients   kinds of chemicals found in food that we need to be healthy

protozoa   single-celled germs that can cause disease in people and other animals

virus   tiny living thing that causes diseases in plants and animals

FURTHER READING

What Does It Mean To Have Allergies? Louise Spilsbury (Heinemann Library, 2002)

Why Does my Body Smell? and other questions about hygiene, Louise Spilsbury (Heinemann Library, 2002)

Why Should I Wash my Hair? and other questions about healthy skin and hair, Louise Spilsbury (Heinemann Library, 2003)

INDEX